£6

The Borough of Havant

in old picture postcards

by
P.N. Rogers

European Library – Zaltbommel/Netherlands

Second edition: 1992

GB   ISBN 90 288 3182 7 / CIP

© 1985 European Library – Zaltbommel/Netherlands

INTRODUCTION

The Borough of Havant — a pictorial contribution to the records of its social history.

The districts comprising the Borough of Havant, were, prior to 1974, collectively known as the Urban District of Havant and Waterloo, a title adopted in 1932, when the geographical boundaries were changed together with the older title of 'Havant Union and Rural District'.

Throughout this book the name Havant will be used only in association with the town of Havant, the remaining locations each retaining their own name and identities, including the districts of Drayton and Farlington prior to 1932. Within the following pages, much of the pertinent information contained in the text associated with each photograph, is freely available in many old documents, newspapers, directories and histories of the districts and, as a consequence, there is no general acknowledgement of sources.

It is hoped that each item of information is indeed correct but that the reader will permit the author's indulgence in any discrepancies which may have occurred. All of the photographs are believed to be out of copyright but where such copyright is in doubt all known sources are acknowledged, and again, it is asked that any inadvertant infringement may be forgiven.

The 1970's and 1980's have proved themselves to be the age of the computer and the age of high technology. A forward looking world contemplates with anticipation each marvel of invention, each new development and each revolutionary contribution to an ever increasing automated society, wherein machines and electronic devices are actually thinking for us and determining our futures. Through these pages the casual historian, the nostalgic adult and the enquiring youngster will realise that the 70's and 80's have also proved to be, more so than at any other period, a time for looking back. The photographic contents of this book are offered as a reminder that progress has always been with us, that man has always been an inventive genius and that time has never stood still.

The many changes, be they for better or worse, that have taken place in our towns and in our times become apparent when comparisons are made with the scenes depicted in the following pictures. Buildings, vehicles and even the street furniture (lamp-posts, railings, signs etc.), show enormous changes. The changing times are also reflected in the clothing of the period.

The early years of the twentieth century are often referred to as 'the good old days'. Good days perhaps there were, but bad days were also ever present, for these were the times of indifferent sanitation, tuberculosis, diphtheria and death among children, contaminated food and water carts to lay the ever present dust in the streets.

The comments accompanying each photograph are intended to be, depending on the readers age, a gentle jolt to the memory or an incentive to enquire more deeply into the historic past of the towns, villages and districts which now comprise the Borough of Havant. The compelling desire to read, watch, listen and involve oneself in all that is history, has resulted in much of the nation's leisure time being given over to historically orientated pursuits; whilst the passion for collecting items of historical interest, curiosity or importance, has prompted the expansion of antique and collecting markets. Booksellers have also enjoyed the increased sales of literature relating to local history.

No attempt is being made in this volume to compete with the many excellent publications which have appeared in recent years. They have, for the most part, dealt thoroughly with the histories of the borough whilst this book of photographs and commentaries has been produced with the intention of bringing to the public a large number of interesting and often rare pictures which depict local scenes and events of yesteryear.

Acknowledgements

Almost all of the pictures reproduced here have been selected from the author's collection but the following have been most kind in making available material which is wholly owned by them. I am particularly grateful to Mrs. M.G. Hayward of Purbrook, Mr. B.C. Pethybridge of Waterlooville and Mr. E. Noel of Widley.

Thanks must also be given to Mr. Pethybridge for his help and advice relating to the Portsdown and Horndean Light Railway. To Mrs. Hayward for being generous in sharing with me her memories of the Purbrook Industrial School and to Mr. T.W. Marshall of Havant, who also contributed to the pictorial content of this book, by allowing me to copy from his own extensive collection. I trust that he will be delighted to see again the photographs as they appear in this volume.

Others deserving of grateful thanks, are the staff of the Local Libraries, Hampshire County Records Office, Portsmouth City Records Office and the Cosham office of the Ordnance Survey for their unfailing tolerance, courtesy, help and advice.

To David and Jennifer Jordan, for their patience in reading and correcting my literary shortcomings, I owe a particular debt of thanks.

Finally, acknowledgement is given to the very many photographers, living or dead, who were responsible for producing the originals of all the photographs and who recorded those times, places and events for us to enjoy in 1985.

Peter Rogers

'What is the use of a book,' thought Alice, *'without pictures or conversations.'*

(Alice in Wonderland)

St. Faith's and West St., Havant.

1. St. Faiths church is the feature of the Havant town centre and is an ancient place of worship dating from circa 1150. Traces of a Roman floor were found in the nineteenth century when restoration work was being undertaken and the crossroads shown in the picture are certain to have been the centre of the settlement in Roman times, the church occupying an identical relative position to that of the Cathedral at Chichester. The horse trough and drinking fountain are shown prior to the erection of the town war memorial which now occupies this corner.

Havant. St. Faith's Church.

2. Dedicated to St. Faith of Aquitaine, the young girl who was martyred in about the year 290, the parish church of Havant has occupied this site since Saxon times although no definite evidence of a Saxon building now remains. Certainly the church was here in the twelfth century and the older parts of its tower can be dated from that period. The postcard shows the nave and the crossing of arches supporting the tower which was partially rebuilt in 1874 when it was discovered to be in a near state of collapse; at about this time the nave was also rebuilt. The chancel seen beyond the crossing is the oldest complete remaining part of the early church and dates from the thirteenth century. The town traditionally celebrated the feast day of St. Faith when a fair was held each October in the nearby fairfield, now the site of Fairfield Road.

3. North Street, from the Havant crossroads, shows the old Church Institute next to the 'White Hart'. The institute buildings, after major alteration, now accommodates a book shop and the offices of a building society, while the shop and houses seen opposite, today comprise the premises of a major bank. Also on the left in the picture is the 'George Inn', now in use as offices.

4. Unfortunately, the circumstances prompting this extravagant display at the premises of J.H. Stubbs in North Street are not known. It does seem, however, to be an exhibition of prizewinning carcases and cuts of meat following a local trade event and Mr. Stubbs and his staff appear proud to be photographed with the results of their labours. The fact that fresh meat was presented to the public in the open air, with all the associated problems of dust, flies and dung polluted streets, shows the almost total lack of concern of both the vendors and customers in the years before the awareness of the need for hygiene.

5. A local phenomenon, the Lavant Stream, occurs at perplexingly uncertain intervals. Rising in the Idsworth area it flows through the Hampshire countryside until it arrives at Havant and the upper reaches of the harbour. Until its course was ducted below ground it would, on occasions, flood North Street to the extent shown in the photograph. The scene looks south from near today's junction with Elm Road.

NORTH ST. HAVANT.

6. An almost identical location to that shown in the previous picture but without the hazard of flooded pavements. The year is 1907 and on the immediate right can be seen the coachworks of Messrs. Liningtons (carriage makers to the gentry since 1811). In later years they became leaders in the motor car world and now trade very successfully in nearby Portsmouth.

Havant.   North Street.

7. The face of North Street has assumed many guises in its lifetime, an example being seen here. This postcard dated 1905, shows a pair of cottages on the right which, after alteration, were for many years the premises of a local butcher. Removed in the 1970's, their site is now part of a parade of modern shops. The brick built house and shop next door remain today as the office and consulting rooms of an optician, but the entire terrace opposite was removed and developed many years ago.

8. The upper part of North Street shows a horse-drawn cab which had probably just left the railway station. Studied carefully, the photograph reveals the steps of the footbridge which accompanied the level crossing at the end of the road. This short section of North Street accommodated four public houses: the 'Six Bells' on the right and the 'Foresters Arms', 'Perseverence' and the 'Star' on the left. Note the inquisitive children including the girl with the large hoop.

9. The 'Foresters Arms', one of the five public houses sited in this street, also incorporated the oyster shop seen in the picture and it is probable that in the days of cheap food and drink, the trades were complementary to each other. The building is no longer part of North Street, but its vacant space is used as a car park almost next door to the 'Perseverence' public house.

North Street & Congregational Church, Havant.

10. The 'Foresters Arms' of the previous picture has, by 1914, become a pair of houses, one of which is also a boot and shoe shop. Its neighbour with the dormer window still exists in Havant's North Street and currently trades as a Chinese 'take-away' food shop. The cottages south of the church have given way to Elm Road but, in this postcard, are part concealing the 'Empire Cinema' which was originally sited here before the present cinema was opened in East Street in 1936.

11. The upper part of North Street with the 'Perseverence' public house on the immediate right, its next door neighbour being the former 'Foresters Arms'. Sited opposite at this time, circa 1910, is the town market which, having had several unsuccessful locations over many years, finally established itself here in the early years of this century and remained in business until the 1950's.

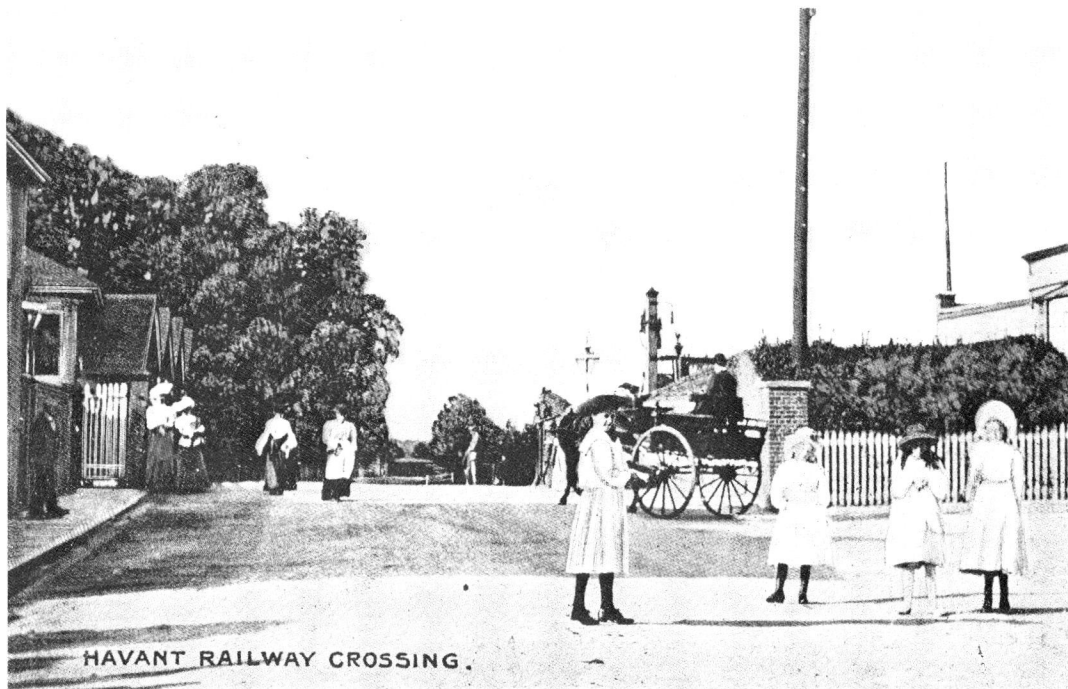

HAVANT RAILWAY CROSSING.

12. The North Street railway crossing in 1906 showing Leigh Road stretching away towards distant Rowlands Castle. This was, of course, the main Havant to London Road and carried coaches, waggons, carts and, by this time, the occasional motor car, though it is doubtful whether in those early years that this crossing experienced the volume of traffic which now occurs daily at the other two crossing barriers which still remain in use locally.

13. Havant railway station in 1927 bears little resemblance to that of the present day. The only features remaining are the New Lane signal box and cottage seen here, left and right in the foreground. The station buildings and platforms were replaced in 1938, and, in more recent years, the coal and goods yards have been closed making provision for a commuters car park. In the distance behind the steam locomotive are the crossing gates which were sited at the upper end of North Street giving access to Leigh Road; the removal of these gates and the subsequent extension of buildings and platforms made each road a cul-de-sac and considerably altered the traffic flow through Havant.

14. This undated postcard of Havant Railway Station taken before the rebuilding of 1938, shows the Hayling Island train standing at the left-hand platform and the crossing gate which gave access to North Street from Leigh Road in the centre of the picture. All the buildings, platforms and canopies seen here were demolished in the pre-war redevelopment.

15. A postcard which has suffered greatly with age shows Havant railway station in 1904. Completed by 1847, it was improved and partially rebuilt in 1889, followed by a complete reconstruction in 1938. Although of a poor quality, this picture is included as an essential contribution to Havant's pictorial past.

16. Until the construction of Park Road South in the years prior to the Second World War, South Street was the only route to Hayling and, consequently, this small thoroughfare carried, for over one hundred years, all the vehicular traffic to and from the island.

17. This largely residential street, now a cul-de-sac, housed three of Havant's public houses, and one of them, 'The Old House at Home', is seen on the left of the picture. Its claim to be the oldest domestic building remaining in Havant is probably correct, although the date of 1339 displayed on its façade almost certainly pre-dates the premises by 200 years. Several buildings in the town contain Tudor work and timber framing but 'The Old House at Home' remains the only structure with a complete outward appearance in the Tudor style.

18. A reverse view of South Street shows 'The Old House at Home' to be a near perfect example of a sixteenth century, timber framed building and, although lacking its original thatched roof, it still remains Havant's most picturesque property. The railings on the right are those which surrounded the graveyard of St. Faith's church which, because of its thousands of burials over many centuries, has gradually assumed a height of, perhaps, one metre or more above the pavements.

19. Part of the town's commercial centre, East Street was, and still is, home to many professions as well as a number of shops and licensed premises. The town's post office was sited here in the early years and was the building which is seen behind the window cleaner's ladder.

East Street, Havant

20. A reverse view of the previous location shows buildings which, in 1985, are almost all still in situ. Some perhaps have had alterations made to the lower shop fronts but evidence of this earlier period can still be seen if one glances at the upper stories.

21. A very old picture of 'The Brown Jug' in East Street, Havant, shows an early steam driven brewers dray on what is obviously delivery day. Note that the wheels on the vehicle are of solid iron and of a type which were used on steam rollers. In later years, the wheels would have had a rubber surface fitted, thus lessening the noise and the wear on the roads. Todays' veteran and vintage vehicle enthusiasts could probably delight in telling us the make of this waggon and, from its number plate, its year of registration.

22. A second, and later, picture of 'The Brown Jug' which although still an early photograph bears little resemblance to the premises shown on the previous page. Gone are the casement windows and the tile-hung frontage, and although basically the same building, the only recognisable feature is the Brown Jug hanging over the pavement. In what was apparently a popular sport at the time, a local cycling organisation is seen meeting at what must have been the club premises, as testified by the shield bearing the letters C.C. displayed on the upper wall.

23. The principal buildings of West Street in 1919 were the Post Office and the Capitol and Counties Bank. In 1985, the public are still being catered for at the bank which has long since changed its name; the Post Office building, however, is now a branch of a national chain of domestic electrical retailers, the G.P.O. having moved to new premises in East Street in 1936. The familiar figure of the duty traffic policeman can be seen near the 'White Hart' public house. He is featured in his white cap and gloves in many photographs of the period, for it must be remembered that this was Havant's major crossroads and, while it appears to be a quiet junction, it became necessary to install traffic lights here in the 1930's.

24. It is probable that the sound of the post-horn was heard here in the nineteenth century when the post coaches bound for Portsmouth and Chichester stopped at the 'Dolphin', a popular coaching inn and hotel. The 'Dolphin' contributed to the character of West Street for at least 150 years until it was demolished to make way for a shopping arcade in 1958. In its heyday the inn boasted extensive stabling and coaching facilities and had its own bowling green.

25. A familiar sight in Havant, the 'Street Parade'. In this instance in 1907, the object is to collect money for the local hospitals. The town fire brigade and police force were always evident at these events and contributed a military thoroughness with their discipline and polished brasswork. It was almost certainly a Sunday when this parade took place judging from the 'Sunday best' clothing worn by all those present.

26. Havant was well known for its parchment making industry. The availability of fresh spring water from the chalk downs and the skins of sheep that grazed on these downs, established the industry in this area as early as Roman times. It is said that Magna Carta was written on Havant parchment. In the picture, skins are being soaked in a lime/water solution, one of the many processes involved in the manufacture of parchment.

27. The demolition of the old 'Town Mill' in 1958, robbed Havant of the last of the many water mills for which the area had long been famous. The mills gradually closed as progressive industrialists introduced machinery and methods which made obsolete the local giants which had contributed to the districts well being for probably a thousand years. Closed in 1934, this mill, together with the mill pond, was finally removed in 1958, to make possible the road improvements necessary to the rapidly growing town of Havant. At the time of writing a very small part of the mill pond still exists near 'The Dolphin' public house and the brickwork which housed the mill wheel and race can be found among the massive bridge building works taking place to create a flyover at the Langstone Roundabout.

WEST ST. HAVANT.

28. Fifty years before the by-pass came to Havant, this was a part of the main east-west road. The house in the immediate right foreground has since gone, making way for the grounds of the Portsmouth Water Company which, together with its modern offices, accounts for much of West Street's south side. The continuing terraces of houses on the right still remain but the pale coloured building seen opposite, which was once Havant's Union Poor House, has, with the adjoining Police Station, long since been removed.

R.C. Church and School Havant

29. The early history of the Roman-Catholic faith in the Havant district is particularly interesting and deserves more space than has been given here. The building of St. Joseph's in West Street was the culmination of two centuries and more of efforts by the Roman-Catholic community to establish for themselves a sound and permanent place of worship. Meetings had been conducted in virtual secrecy in the early years and there is evidence that as late as 1733, upper floors of adjoining cottages at Langstone had been fashioned into a chapel. This was followed, again in the eighteenth century, by a move to Brockhampton where, similarly, cottages were converted to form a chapel. These premises however, were soon outgrown and a conventional mission was built. With a continually growing population, there was eventually a need to establish a larger church in the district and St. Joseph's, with its adjoining presbytery and school for sixty pupils, was built in 1875.

30. This postcard, dated Christmas 1910, complements the photograph on the previous page and is a delightful study of the period, showing clergy leaving St. Joseph's Roman-Catholic church in Havant.

31. Leigh Park, once a large country estate but sold to Portsmouth Corporation for development as a new town in post-war years, was the seat of Sir George Staunton. It was a later owner, however, William Stone, who had this mansion built in 1863. The grounds had been designed and landscaped by Sir George and became what could only be described as a Botanical Garden, containing trees, shrubs and plant specimens from all over the world. The lake contained artificial islands together with ornamental bridges, and the random buildings within the grounds depicted the styles of China, Turkey, Ancient Greece etc. The house shown in this picture was demolished in 1959 but the very attractive gardens are open to the public and contain among other things an educational farm trail where rare species of domestic farm animals may be seen.

BEDHAMPTON CROSSING.

32. This situation, while probably not uncommon in 1906, would not be allowed to take place today, for although the crossing is still in use, it has a continental barrier system which would allow livestock to scatter along the live rails if panicked. The farm cart seen in the background is possibly making for the 'Golden Lion' where the driver could indulge in a liquid lunch? – the shadows indicate that it is probably midday!

33. New Road, Bedhampton, narrow by today's standards, was built, at his own expense, by Sir George Staunton, the owner of the Leigh Park Estate, probably to relieve the tedium of being forced to travel through the streets of Havant and then having to wait to negotiate the railway crossing pictured here. The motor vehicles in the background, although indistinct, are of a 1930 vintage and the horse-drawn bakers cart is delivering bread for its owners Messrs. Smith and Vosper of Portsmouth.

34. Public houses and church buildings then, as now, often appear to be placed close together; a moral judgement on each other perhaps, in the days of the temperance movements at the turn of the century. Bedhampton's main road, over a very short distance, could boast several of each, and although the 'Wheelwrights Arms' shown here has long since ceased to trade, the 'Golden Lion' on the far side of the church remains today as a licensed house.

J.T. Coldman. Main Road, Bedhampton. 6079

35. Viewed from the opposite direction, and at a later date, the 'Golden Lion' is the only public house now in sight. The 'Wheelwrights' has removed its sign and become a private dwelling thus making the distant 'Belmont' the next oasis for the thirsty traveller.

THE OLD MILL, BEDHAMPTON

36. The old Bedhampton Mill was sited a short distance north of the present Bedhampton to Havant by-pass. Although it was demolished many years ago, its mill house can still be seen alongside of the watercourse which provided its motive power. There has been a long tradition of milling locally and at one time Bedhampton could boast two corn mills and a fulling mill. The district is very well served with freshwater springs and the Portsmouth Water Company gather much of their supply from the area.

37. Visitors to 'The Elms' at Bedhampton could be forgiven for thinking that this was the Manor House. Its rather grand appearance makes it the most impressive building in the village, containing as it does a diversity of styles quite out of keeping with the local architecture. It was the home of Sir Theophilus Lee who, it is claimed, was a relation of the Duke of Wellington. Relation or mere friend, this national hero is said to have been entertained here following his success at Waterloo. The family chapel, which had been designed by the Adam Brothers in 1760, was converted for the occasion and the beautiful 'Waterloo Room' as it was called is now a feature of the house. (The Manor House in its traditional English country style is a near neighbour of 'The Elms'.)

38. Constructed in the first half of the twelfth century, the Church of St. Thomas probably replaced the Saxon centre of worship which was known to have existed in Bedhampton at the time of the Domesday Survey of 1086. The chancel arch is the oldest remaining feature of the Norman building, the chancel itself being rebuilt and extended in the thirteenth and fourteenth centuries; it is possible, also, that the nave contains some elements of the Norman period. In 1982 the village celebrated what was considered to be the 850th anniversary of the present church.

39. A short distance from Bedhampton village on the lower slopes of Portsdown Hill is this fortress like house 'The Towers'. Previously called 'Belmont Castle' a Havant street directory for 1926 reports that Queen Elizabeth slept here on several occasions. Whilst that claim must be in doubt it would at least account for the appearance of a 'Tower of London' type building in rural Hampshire!

Belmont House, Bedhampton, N.r Havant.

40. Like its near neighbour 'The Towers', 'Belmont House' also boasted a royal visitor, for it is claimed that Queen Victoria stayed here when young. Belmont Park's most well-known claim to fame was during the Second World War when it became host to the Royal Navy. The grounds provided hutted accommodation for the overcrowded and bomb damaged naval establishments of the area.

The Lodge Gates, Belmont House, Nr Havant.

41. The gates and lodge to the Belmont Park Estate stood near to the present Maylands Road and very close to the new 'Belmont' public house. The Lodge, and indeed Belmont House itself, have been demolished in the development of Bedhampton and a modern housing estate has taken their place swallowing up the adjoining park and farmlands.

42. The lower slopes of Bedhampton Hill present a lazy summer picture of a scene long past. The original 'Belmont' public house was the last building on the left and Coldmans Store and Post Office, the larger property on the right. The wall and trees in the centre of the picture are obscuring the gates and lodge of 'Belmont Park'.

Bedhampton Village.

43. Brookside Road in 1911, is viewed from its junction with Bedhampton Hill. Unfortunately, the thatched cottages which contributed to this rural scene have long since been removed, as has Coldman's corner shop which was demolished in 1971. A forward looking Havant Borough has since declared Old Bedhampton to be a conservation area with the hope that the village will now remain undisturbed by any future planning.

44. An oasis on the Havant to Portsmouth Road was this spot at the foot of the Portsdown and Bedhampton Hills, adjacent to the old 'Belmont' public house. Here, both horses and drivers could rest and satisfy their thirst before tackling the long haul to Portsmouth or perhaps to the top of Portsdown Hill. Coldman's shop and Post Office can be seen opposite on the corner of Brookside Road.

Farlington Church, near Portsmouth.

iwa 1762

45. The Church of St. Andrew at Farlington, pictured here in 1905, served a community stretching from the shores of Langstone Harbour, north over Portsdown to Waterlooville. Until the building of St. George's at Waterlooville in 1831 and St. John's at Purbrook, which was consecrated in 1858, parishioners from these rural areas would have had to attend services at Farlington. The situation was further eased in 1874, when John Deverell of Purbrook funded the building of Christchurch at Portsdown. Unbelievably, the road seen in this postcard view was, until the building of the Farlington by-pass in the 1960's, the main south coast road.

Main Road, Drayton, near Cosham.

46. Havant Rural District's influence over Drayton and Farlington extended, until 1932, as far as this point on the A27 road. The 'New Inn', seen on the right, faces a terrace of shops which, in a different guise, still form part of Drayton's shopping centre. Drayton Lane is the obscure turning near the row of white posts and it was this lane, reaching both up and down Portsdown Hill which marked the boundary between Portsmouth and the Havant Union and Rural District. At the time that this postcard was produced in 1914, the Borough of Portsmouth was contained within the Island of Portsea and did not extend its boundaries to include Cosham until 1920. It was twelve years later, on 1st April 1932, that the City of Portsmouth established its new and present boundary near Rectory Avenue in Farlington.

47. Farlington Railway station was the scene of this crash in July 1894, when the coaches of a westbound train ran into its derailed brake van, killing the guard and injuring several passengers. The station had been built to serve the Portsmouth Park Racecourse which was opened in 1891.

48. Built in 1891, this was the grandstand of the 'Portsmouth Park Club', a large racecourse which was established on the marshes of Drayton and Farlington. The site of the grandstand can be located at the lower end of Station Road, Drayton, just over the railway line where a footbridge gave access to Farlington railway station and the racecourse. The course had mixed fortunes over the years until it was taken over by the War Department in 1915 for use as an ammunition dump and vehicle park. Racing never again took place here, so bringing to an end Havant's association with the 'sport of kings'.

49. The 'Oyster House', built in 1819, near Ware Point on the Farlington Marshes, was home to the Russell family who were well known oyster fishermen in Langstone Harbour. The property, which was also known locally as the 'Black House' or the 'Lone House', occupied almost all of the tiny off shore island on which it was built. The picture illustrates the almost total lack of foreshore surrounding the building and the attempts which were made to fend off the ravages of high water with wooden stakes almost in the form of a palisade. Damaged by a German bomb during the Second World War, the house was finally demolished in about 1950. The Russell family had a virtual monopoly of the local shell fish industry. They owned two houses at the Milton Locks in Portsmouth and were the proprietors of the 'Winkle Market' in Langstone High Street.

50. In 1932, the Portsdown Petrol Filling station at Widley had the appearance of a film set in a developing Texan township! It was, and still is in its modern form, sited on the A3 on the northern slopes of Portsdown Hill. In those early years, petrol was hand cranked into the glass containers at the top of these 'lighthouse like' dispensers, then delivered by gravity into the customers motor cars. If the cost of petrol was too prohibitive, one could always board the local tramcar which conveniently passed the garage!

51. Commencing in 1903, the Portsdown and Horndean Light Railway ran a service from Cosham to Horndean and although it was proposed to extend the routes to both Petersfield and Hambledon these plans were never carried through. This photograph taken in 1903, shows car number five in mint condition, complete with curtains and newly decorated body panels in the company colours of cream and emerald green. There was seating for 21 in the lower saloon and 33 on the top deck.

52. This incident, south of Purbrook village, illustrates the problem faced by other road users when confronted by a P. & H.L.R. tramcar. The track between Waterlooville and Portsdown lay in the middle of the highway and dominated the road, sometimes to the exclusion of other vehicles. Here, however, the limited width of the road is sufficient and the situation is not as hazardous as it looks.

Stakes Hill Road, Purbrook.

53. This unusual building, 'Fir Lodge', can still be seen at the junction of Stakes Road, Ladybridge Road and Park Avenue, but the country lane has now become a major road serving the built up area which was once a beautiful part of Purbrook. The house has a strange story in that it was once a chapel built by Squire Deverell in an ecclesiastical feud between the Reverend Richards of Farlington and himself. Christchurch, at Portsdown, was later endowed by Deverell as a direct result of the bitterness which existed between the two men.

54. Purbrook Park House, photographed in 1930, was built as a country seat for John Deverell and replaced an earlier property, which had been built in 1770. The estate purchased in 1837 and developed by Squire Deverell amounted to about 600 acres and the new house was its hub having three carriage drives approaching from different directions. Built during a period when classical styles were being re-introduced, the façade and portico with its Grecian columns, imitates almost exactly Rookesbury Park House at Wickham. Deverell's Mansion is, today, Purbrook Park School.

At Purbrook.

55. Purbrook takes its name from the stream which runs under the main road at this bridge, just south of the village centre. The origin of the name is probably Anglo Saxon and is generally accepted to mean, 'Brook of the Water Sprite'. The stream, which goes on to swell the waters of the minor River Wallington, is today culverted under the present road and passes very near to the major roundabout, which has been created at the new junction with Ladybridge Road.

St. John the Baptist's, Purbrook.

56. Purbrook's Church of St. John the Baptist is clearly seen in this postcard view of 1910. It would not be possible to record the same scene today for, from this angle, the building is now partially obscured by mature trees and the lych gate, which was erected as a memorial to those local folk who gave their lives in the First World War. Commenced in 1843, the church was not consecrated until 1858 due, in part, to the continued ill feeling between the Reverend E.T. Richards of Farlington and John Deverell of Purbrook.

57. The original 'Woodman' public house, seen here in Purbrook village in 1912, was originally a lodge house of the Purbrook Manor Estate. Sited almost next door to the old vicarage and opposite St. John's Church, it was an attractive feature of the village until its demolition. Its successor now stands 100 yards further south.

58. Travelling south through Purbrook village and approaching the old post office building is car number one of the P. & H.L.R. The tramcar carries no advertising on its front upper facia so is probably still fairly new which will date this photograph to about 1905. Happily, the buildings to the left of Post Office Road are still part of the local scene, although those on the right have been replaced by others which are far less imposing.

59. Children and staff of the Purbrook Church of England School, photographed at about the turn of the century. Probably their first appearance before a camera, best clothes were obviously called for, as is apparent from the boy's smart suits and the girl's pinafores and lace.

60. Purbrook was fortunate in having John Deverell as the local squire and lord of the manor. This philanthropic gentleman endowed several institutions in the district, including, in 1868, the Purbrook Industrial School for Boys which remained under the Deverell control until 1912 when the entire establishment, together with 17 acres of land, was given as a gift to the Hampshire County Council by William Deverell, the son of the founder. The first Industrial Schools were permitted by statute in 1857 'for the better training of vagrant children' and gave power to the justices to commit children to Industrial Schools which were to be certified by the Secretary of State.

61. At Purbrook Industrial School, boys wore uniform, had their own band and were taught the rudiments of military drill and exercise. An inspector's report for 1900 notes that 37 'Old Boys' were known to have taken part in engagements in the South African War. The school was in no way a military institution however, for among the skills which were taught there were tailoring, bread-making, shoemaking, blacksmithing, animal husbandry and farming.

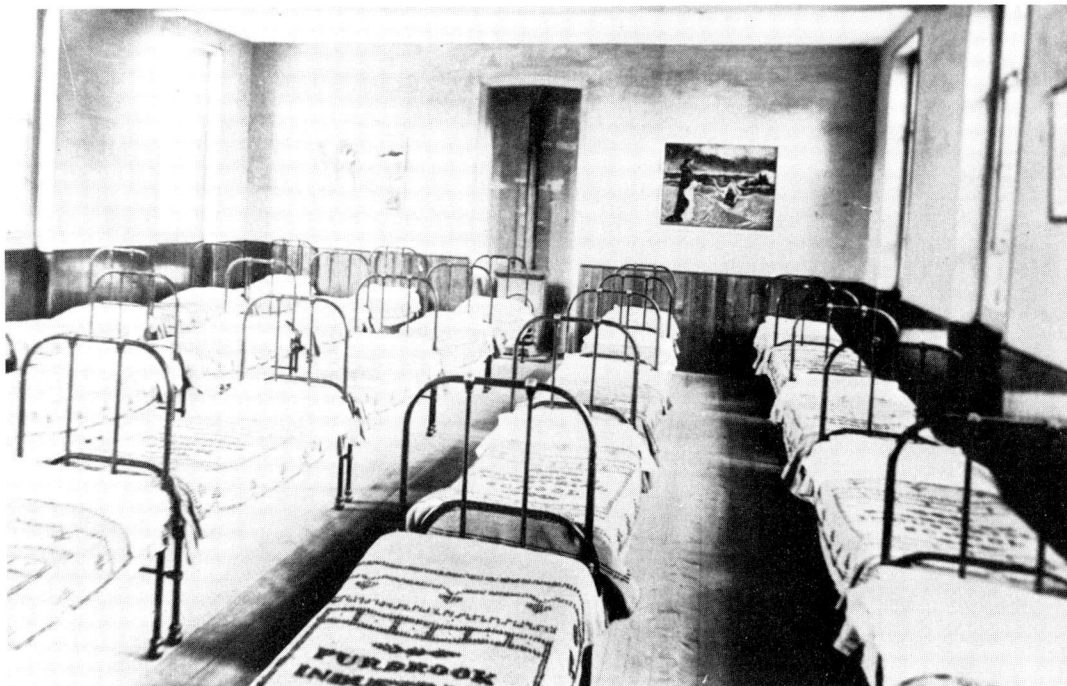

62. This photograph of the school dormitory presents a stark picture of the most basic accommodation with apparently no other furniture than beds. One wonders if perhaps an adjoining locker room held any possessions which the boys may have had?

63. The meals provided at the school were of the most uninteresting fare lacking variety and imagination. The same meals, repeated several times in any one week, never included pudding or cake of any kind, whilst jam did not appear on the menu until well into the twentieth century. Portraits of Their Majesties grace the walls of the dining room together with a picture showing the might of Britain's Navy.

64. This delightful little building, now lost to Purbrook, was the chapel and school room of the Industrial School. The boys who were admitted to the institution, from the age of six years, attended regular classes which started at 7.00 a.m. Normally rising at 6.30 a.m., a concession was permitted on Sundays when the time was extended to 7.00 a.m.

65. Staff of the Industrial School are pictured here with (seated centre) Mr. A. Fielder, a local farmer and nurseryman, who, in 1900, was the school superintendent. In 1912, the first year in which the school was managed by the County Authority, there were employed two members of teaching staff, six members of industrial training staff, a matron and a bandmaster-cum-gymnasium instructor. This made ten people in all who were paid a combined salary of £670. per annum.

66. The final photograph in this series of Purbrook Industrial School shows part of the main block which comprised the boy's hostel and staff housing. Built around a quadrangle, it provided a paved area within, which could be used for assembly or drill purposes. Other buildings nearby were for schooling, craft instruction and farm stock, whilst, within a short distance, were the houses provided for the remaining staff and their families. The establishment was closed when the school was evacuated to North Wales shortly after the start of the Second World War, and was demolished in later years as part of Purbrook's development.

67. Members of the Purbrook Primitive Methodist Church are seen here whilst on a visit to the Isle of Wight in 1902. The first meeting of the Methodists in Purbrook took place on the local common in 1877 and it was John Deverell who backed their cause by allowing them to use his premises in Stakes Road (now April Cottage) and a large marquee which he made available. In the following year, 1878, a permanent chapel was built in the London Road and this remained their home until the present church was opened in Stakes Road in 1932.

68. A postcard dated 1917 looks north toward the cross roads in Waterlooville and illustrates how development has greatly affected the appearance of this section of the London Road. In 1985, the shop with the sunblinds, together with its neighbouring house, are all that remain of the left hand terrace, the Queen's Temperance Hotel and the Baptist Church having been demolished. On the opposite side of the road the only buildings still retaining an original profile are those in the tall block adjacent to the passing tramcar, the others having been removed or altered to form a terrace of modern shops, restaurants and offices.

69. A gentle way of life is pictured here in 1910 and it seems almost a tragedy that this, the centre of Waterlooville, has been re-developed to such a degree that very little is recognisable in 1985. The old 'Heroes of Waterloo' public house has gone and in its place stands the modern premises of the National Westminster Bank. On the opposite corner of Hambledon Road and behind the wheels of the brake, the grocer's shop, together with its neighbour the Baptist Church, have been replaced by 'Clock House', a large block of shops and offices. The terrace in the left foreground together with much more, which disappointedly is not shown here, is almost entirely taken up by the chain stores of Tesco, Woolworths, Boots, etc. and the road is now a pedestrian precinct.

St.Georges,Waterlooville.

70. The Church of St. George lies a few yards inside the Hambledon Road from the old village crossroads and was built in 1831 on land which had been given by Mr. T. Thistlewayte of Southwick. Prior to this date, devoted parishioners had to trudge through the lanes and over the hill to St. Andrews at Farlington. In 1834 the parish register noted that the name of the village is Waterlooville but from at least 1847 the 'ville' has been dropped and does not appear again until 1870.

71. Sundays in Waterlooville, given fine weather, meant that the boys of the Purbrook Industrial School would march with their band to and from Christchurch at Portsdown. Passing through the centre of the town to the curiosity of the onlookers, they were for many years a feature of the local sabbath forming the choir in the church in addition to entertaining with the band which was led by Mr. Kent. The shop with the sunblinds open is on the corner of Stakes Hill Road and London Road and today is the premises of Lloyds Bank.

Stakes Hill Road, Waterlooville.

72. Beyond these houses lie the open spaces of the countryside, for in 1912 Waterlooville came to an end here and the traveller would then pass only the occasional dwelling before reaching the hamlet of Stakes, so named after the De-Stakes family who were the local lords in the thirteenth century. Before that time, the district was known as Frendstaple, and it is pleasing to note that this ancient name has been re-introduced in the new housing estate recently built.

Stakes Hill.

Photo and Published by H. Marshall, Waterlooville.

73. Stakes Hill Post Office, which stood almost opposite the 'Fox and Hounds' public house, was probably an original farm building which had been added to over several generations. The stucco wall covering could perhaps be concealing a basic timber framing which would have fairly positively dated the property. Whatever its age, the building has, alas, been demolished, although in this, a more enlightened era, it would certainly have been the subject of a conservation order thus ensuring its continued existence.

74. 'Oaklands', at Stakes, was the home, until his death in 1853, of General Sir Charles Napier hero of the Peninsular and India Wars. Sir Charles was a descendant of John Napier, Laird of Merchiston Castle near Edinburgh, and a cousin to Admiral Sir Charles Napier, whose country seat was at Merchistoun Hall, Horndean. 'Oaklands', now greatly enlarged with additional buildings, is today a well-known Roman-Catholic School and possesses a particularly fine concert hall which has become a mecca for devotees of serious music.

COWPLAIN. FROM PARK LANE.

75. This location is now Cowplain's busy shopping centre. The houses remain but have been converted into business premises. A modern supermarket and bank take the place of the old tram shed which dominated this terrace for probably sixty years. The postcard, dated 1909, shows Park Lane, once known as Bedhampton Lane, which before the construction of the A3M motorway could take the adventurous traveller on a cross country route to Havant and Leigh Park, emerging by design or coincidence near to Park Lane, Bedhampton.

Cowplain

76. By the year 1920, the previous scene has altered a little to include Cowplain post office. The pony and trap shown waiting here could barely cope with today's heavy traffic on this, the busy A3, with its associated yellow road markings and pedestrian crossings.

77. A growing estate, with its increasing population, encouraged the owner to further expand, and here is seen a much enlarged post office in London Road, Cowplain. Note the many advertising signs on the forecourt and shop front. Enamelled signs are today sought after by collectors of nostalgia and because of their often brilliant colours and glazed surfaces are known as 'Street Jewellery'.

78. Prior to the re-alignment of the parish and statutory boundaries, Cowplain was in the district of Catherington. In those early years, the nearest places of worship were the churches at Catherington, Blendworth and Waterlooville. It was no surprise, then, when the free and non-conformist religions established themselves in the rural areas, the Cowplain Mission Hall being an example of their willingness to integrate. The growth of the district and with it the need for large community places of worship made this mission hall obsolete, and surprisingly, in 1985, the premises are in use as a boutique and hairdressing salon.

COWPLAIN.

79. The Mission Hall on the previous page is shown again in an earlier postcard, dated 1912. The building can now be seen in the rural setting of the early part of the century with a car of the P. & H.L.R. on a 'passing loop' section of the line.

London Road, Cowplain.

80. Silvesters Garage on the London Road at Cowplain was an oasis to passing motorists in the early 1930's. The road, built surprisingly wide for the period, carried all of the London to Portsmouth traffic, while the local tramway had its track running on the grass verge on the eastern side of the carriageway for the entire route from Waterlooville to Horndean. The garage premises are now the site of a massive, modern petrol filling station which, with its up to date computerised dispensing equipment, is a far cry from the hand wound petrol pumps which were then a feature of the original garage.

The Spotted Cow, Cowplain.

81. This postcard shows the original 'Spotted Cow' public house at Cowplain before its demolition in the 1930's. The name of the village is reputed to have been derived from the local inn, coupled with the fact that in country parlance the extensive tract of land hereabouts is indeed a 'plain'.

THE CROSS ROADS.
WOODLANDS NEAR HAVANT.

82. This very attractive little house was part of the South Leigh Estate owned by Sir Dymoke White. It still stands today on the Emsworth to Rowlands Castle road and serves as offices for its present owners, the Plessey Company. The White family are best remembered as the 'Whites' of Timothy White and Taylors who started their nationwide chain of retail hardware and chemist stores in nearby Portsmouth in 1848, from whence the company grew to own an empire of more than 600 stores.

83. On 22nd June 1911 Emsworth, in keeping with the rest of Great Britain, celebrated the coronation of King George V. The day turned out to be disappointingly wet and the outdoor events were either marred by the weather or cancelled. North Street was decorated for the occasion and the flags and bunting made a brave attempt to colour a drab scene. Anticipating a busy day, the 'Milkmans Arms' public house is having a delivery from a steam driven brewers dray. The two shops in the picture still exist today and trade as a wool shop and a coffee shop.

NORTH STREET, EMSWORTH.

84. An alternative view of North Street, this time looking south. The shop seen on the corner of Palmers Road is still trading today, 75 years after this postcard was produced. Sadly, however, the entire terrace of interesting old buildings which are its neighbours has been replaced with modern premises. In contrast, the elegant parade of shops opposite has been allowed to remain and still contributes to the busy atmosphere of Emsworth's North Street.

85. This view of Emsworth High Street in 1913, is a charming character study of the period, indicating a more relaxed way of life than that of today. Gas lamps, horse-drawn vehicles and then, as now, the ladies finding time to stop and gossip. In 1985 the Crown Hotel, an original coaching inn, is still the dominant building in the left hand terrace, though it now lacks the impressive portico which was its principal feature.

THE SQUARE & HIGH STREET, EMSWORTH.

86. A variation on the previous picture is this view taken from the edge of the square and looking north along the High Street, where the Crown Hotel with its columned porch can be seen. In 1985 the facing terrace remains mostly unaltered with the exception of the 'Ship Inn' which has been given a modern façade. Many postcard views of the Emsworth town centre were produced and, almost always, the photographer has attracted a small crowd. One wonders whether these early photographs were contrived to include the locals, or perhaps the presence of a camera had a magnetic influence?

The Square, Emsworth.

87. This view shows Emsworth's 'Pavilion' Cinema whose current programme includes Harold Lloyd in 'Movie Crazy'. The cinema building started life in 1789 as St. Peters Chapel of Ease; previous to this, worshippers had to attend the Church of St. Thomas á Becket at Warblington. St. Peters later became the Town Hall, and in the cinema boom, 'The Pavilion'. Today it is the store and offices of a local builders merchant. The church seen behind the bus was built as the Primitive Methodist Church in 1877 and now serves as the Emsworth Pastoral Centre.

88. The gentleman seated centre was 'Birkey' Miller, a well-known local character, who together with his tame duck and heron were to be seen daily in and around the town in Emsworth. Ducks are often domesticated in this way but how 'Birkey' managed to tame his heron is a mystery, the answer to which we shall probably never know. Looking closely at the bird, it seems to be offering its master a twig for nest building! The buildings in this picture appear not to have altered over fifty years. The 'Black Dog' public house, however, has suffered a name change and is now 'The Smugglers'.

EMSWORTH HARBOUR

89. A particularly pleasant view of Emsworth shows its houses bordering onto the northern reaches of the harbour and a variety of local boats, probably about to take advantage of the high tide to be off fishing. These were the days when Emsworth's economy depended largely on its fishing and oyster industry. The Emsworth Brewery, long since closed, is the tall structure on the left, with the old 'Anchor' public house standing before it.

QUEEN ST. EMSWORTH.

90. Looking along this slightly downhill road towards the bridge and mill ponds, it is difficult to realise that until recently this was the main and only road through Emsworth to Chichester and beyond. Queen Victoria is said to have travelled this way en route to Portsmouth, hence Queen Street. Happily the changes have been few here, and in 1985 the buildings remain much as they are seen in this postcard view.

The Round House, Emsworth.

91. Emsworth has the distinction of having one foot in each of two counties, Hampshire and West Sussex, the county boundary dividing the town. The Round House, although now demolished, was situated at the southern end of the mill pond and was, of course, in West Sussex.

92. Another West Sussex location, the subject is Lumley Mill, built on the eastern side of the River Ems. Lumley, today, remains a tiny detached community which has somehow managed to preserve its identity. Almost a hamlet in its own right, it is hoped that it can remain remote and unspoiled.

Warblington Castle. Emsworth.

93. It was Margaret, Countess of Salisbury, who, in the early years of the sixteenth century, built Warblington Castle on what was already an ancient site. Certainly the Romans were here and later came the Saxons who created a settlement which was to last until the thirteenth century when Emsworth became the principal local village. King Henry VIII conferred upon Margaret the title of Countess of Salisbury, yet it was he who subsequently ordered her execution when she refused to abandon her Catholic ideals. The story is well-known of her obstinacy on the scaffold when she, rejecting the order to kneel at the block, had her head severed with several hacking blows whilst still on her feet. Vandalising bands of Cromwell's soldiers demolished the castle during the Civil War, leaving only one turret standing gaunt against the sky; pointing like a recriminating finger!

94. Originally dedicated to St. Mary, Warblington's Church of St. Thomas á Becket is, in part pre-Conquest and as such can claim to be the oldest building in the Borough. Several building styles contribute to its structure and, remarkably, some of the Saxon work is found only in the upper levels, the lower Saxon sections being removed and cleverly replaced by the later builders. In the graveyard are two small buildings of unusual design and use. They were built to conceal the watchmen who were employed to protect the newly buried dead from the bodysnatchers; these, the 'Resurrectionists', stole corpses which they then sold to students of anatomy for dissection and research.

48820. HAVANT. THE GREEN POND.

95. This minor junction on the Emsworth Road, near Warblington village, was also the site of the forge and the Green Pond. The road was, until the building of the Havant by-pass in 1965, the main route to Chichester and Brighton. A turning to the left leads to Denvilles, Havant's residential suburb, and to Warblington railway halt, which is a stopping place on the Chichester to Portsmouth line. The forge is now the site of a modern shop and the pond has become a very attractive garden area.

GREEN POND, HAVANT.

96. This delightful Edwardian scene shows the Green Pond in earlier days when it was obviously a much cherished feature of Warblington village. Probably an attraction on a local country walk and no more than one mile from Havant town centre, it would have been a popular spot to visit on summer weekends.

THE MOTOR HALT, WARBLINGTON

97. In the early years of the twentieth century, the London Brighton and South Coast Railway introduced a commuter service between Chichester and Portsmouth. In addition to the regular stations en route, railway halts were also established. A stopping service of locomotives, known as 'Motor Trains', was introduced and the extra stops were called Motor Halts. Warblington, with its growing residential district of Denvilles, became one of these selected stops and the Warblington Motor Halt pictured on this postcard came into existence.

Langstone Road, Havant.

98. In 1915, the main road to Hayling Island was adequate for the relatively few vehicles which would have used it. The toll gate at Hayling's road bridge was located at the Langstone shore and, together with the local railway crossing, was responsible for the massive traffic queues which were experienced with the growing popularity of the motor car in the 1930's.

99. One of the familiar 'Hayling Billy' steam locomotives is seen near Langstone village in the 1930's pulling a mixture of both passenger carriages and goods trucks. These sturdy little tank engines with their tall funnels proved themselves to be one of the most successful locomotives ever built and several are still to be discovered running on the privately owned railways which are encouraged and maintained by Britain's rail enthusiasts. (Photo: Courtesy Lens of Sutton.)

100. This postcard of Langstone High Street dated 1912, shows cattle being driven towards the shore and probably taking a short cut from west of the village to pastures which lay along the coast on the Warblington side of Langstone. In 1985, the traffic which had frequently blocked this little street en route to the local inn 'The Royal Oak', has now been restricted, enabling the village to regain some of its former character.

101. Arriving at this point from mainland Havant all vehicles were obliged to stop and pay the bridge toll. Because the original wooden structure was not intended to accommodate heavy loads, bus passengers had to walk across, rejoining their transport at the other end. Likewise, petrol tankers delivering fuel to the islands garages had to be of a smaller capacity and of a lesser weight than those in general use, thus restricting the quantity of petrol which could be delivered to any one location. This postcard however, shows a Pratts Oil Company vehicle delivering petrol in two gallon cans. Older readers will recall motor spirit being sold by this method at garages before the introduction of petrol pumps and underground storage tanks.

Langston, Havant.

102. A sideways glance from the previous location would have presented the traveller with this view of the Langstone shore. The scene, always popular with photographers and painters, has changed little over the years, the principal exception being the windmill which has now been capped and converted into a private dwelling. The name Langstone is said by some to be taken from 'Longstone' and that buried in the mud nearby is an 'erratic', an ice age boulder jettisoned, perhaps, 100,000 years ago from a prehistoric ice floe.

The old Mill. Langston. Havant.

103. The long abandoned Langstone windmill is seen here in 1911 twenty or more years before its restoration. It has been suggested that from its origins in the early eighteenth century it remained in use until the end of the nineteenth century. Its neglected appearance here would seem to contradict that belief for in addition to the loss of its sails and cap it shows evidence of very many years of neglect and exposure to the elements. Happily it experienced its renaissance in the 1930's and is now a modern and unique house.

LANGSTON SWING BRIDGE, CONNECTING HAYLING ISLAND WITH THE MAIN LAND—OPEN FOR THE PASSAGE OF VESSELS.

Waterlow & Sons Ltd

104. A short distance west of the road bridge to Hayling was the railway bridge. Opened in 1867, the Hayling Railway Company ran a local line from Havant to South Hayling with stopping places en route. The bridge was required to provide access for shipping between the two harbours of Langstone and Chichester. A 30 foot gap in its structure could be created with this swinging centre section, the gears of which were worked by hand. The bridge was used after the railways closure in 1963 as a convenient 'platform' for local fishermen but was dismantled after being rendered unsafe by vandals.

North Hayling Church.

105. St. Peters at Northney, the parish church of North Hayling, is the older of the island's two churches. Built in the twelfth century, it still retains the simple appearance of an ancient English church, although evidence can be seen of structural alterations which took place in the thirteenth and fourteenth centuries. Unique in that its walls apparently have no foundations, it has been buttressed on at least two occasions to keep the structure from collapsing. Large 'erratic' boulders from the last ice age, and at one time common throughout the district, have been used to support both the walls and the internals pillars of the building. St. Peter's three bells, cast in about 1350, claim to be the oldest peal of bells in England.

Monlas Cottage, Hayling Island.

106. The delightful building seen here, 'Monlas Cottage', was unfortunately burnt down in 1921 and only fragments of the original remain today in the present building of that name. On the supposed evidence, a building date of 1486 has been suggested and until its destruction it was considered to be the oldest house on Hayling Island. It was also probably the 'Parish House' referred to in old documents and therefore the home of the Reverend Matthew Monlas who held the Hayling living for many years until his death in 1703.

107. Time passes almost without notice here in North Hayling, for in the 75 years since this postcard was produced the scene is virtually unchanged. Just south of Northney, this terrace remains substantially unaltered, although the village shop has lost its identity by becoming one more house in the row. The quiet lane still winds its way through the Hayling countryside emerging in the equally unspoiled, but traffic conscious village of Stoke.

WATER WORKS, HAYLING ISLAND.

108. In 1895 the South Hayling Water Company Limited, undertook to supply the southern half of the island with piped water, the source being a well at Stoke. A pumping house and water tower were built and shortly after in 1898, the supply was extended to include the rest of the island. With the further development of the area, the Havant Rural District Council arranged, in 1924, for the supply to come from the Portsmouth Water Company on the mainland and trunk mains were installed. The Water Tower, so long a local landmark, was demolished in 1952 but the pumping house still stands and accommodates an automatic booster unit.

The Post Office, Stoke, Hayling.

109. Stoke is a small community clustered around the only through road on the island and is possibly the oldest continuously inhabited settlement. The buildings shown here are still to be found at Hayling's most dangerous road bend. That they have escaped the planner's knife thus far is indeed fortunate, for plans are now afoot to create a much needed by-pass for the village.

49 – Stoke, Hayling Island.

110. Forge Cottage, on the corner of Copse Lane, still bears witness to the fact that here were the forge and workshops of 'The Smithy of Stoke'. No longer does the hammer swing or the anvil ring, but his premises still remain tucked away beside this house in Stoke Village and are probably unnoticed by the thousands who pass this way daily!

The Pound .S. Hayling.

111. In ancient times, almost every parish or manor in the land had its 'pound', an enclosure in which were impounded any livestock found wandering. The owners when claiming their beasts had to pay a fine to secure their release. Usually a scale of fines existed, set against the duration of stay and the type of creature held, cattle, sheep, pigs, etc. In addition to exercising greater control over the local strays, the scheme produced yet another form of income for the parish or the manorial lord, and would also have provided the wages of the 'pinder' or 'poundkeeper'. The remains of Hayling's Pound can be found today in Manor Road opposite the entrance to Church Road. In the postcard, a man can be seen sitting on the gate of the pound.

Manor House, Hayling

112. The Manor House was built in 1777, by the then Duke of Norfolk on a particularly ancient, moated site which had a history dating back many centuries to at least the Norman Period. One theory which has been seriously considered is that this was a possible location of the island's ancient priory.

113. St. Mary's in South Hayling, built in the thirteenth century, is larger and less isolated than its sister church in Northney. Lacking the simplicity of St. Peter's, it embodies the varying styles of many centuries and is, therefore, of greater interest to the serious student of church architecture. St. Mary's once possessed an ancient set of bells, one of which was dated 1324. Regretfully, they were sold in 1805, the year of Trafalgar, to cover the cost of repairs to the church. St. Mary's was long thought to have been the middle of three ancient churches on the island, the third and most southerly being engulfed by the sea together with massive tracts of land in the thirteenth and fourteenth centuries. Legend has been converted into fact in the last twenty years and convincing evidence has been recovered from Hayling Bay where, at a distance of a mile and a half from the shore, stonework has been recovered from the location traditionally known as 'Church Rocks'.

Gable Head, Hayling Island.

114. The small district which is situated where Elm Grove and Church Road meet, is Hayling's 'Gable Head'. It is unlikely that many folk today could correctly place this view, which has since been altered beyond recognition. The local Co-op store has been replaced by large modern premises and, sadly, the other buildings no longer exist. This once quiet rural road, is now home to many shops, the Fire Station, Hayling's Public Library, bus garage and local public house. The district has been further added to with the establishment of Chinese and Indian restaurants and 'take-away' shops, a far step from this Hayling of yester-year!

ELM GROVE, SOUTH HAYLING

115. A much later view of Elm Grove looking back towards 'Gable Head'. The houses have for the most part, been converted into shops, and the field on the left is now host to the Public Library, Fire Station and a public house the 'Hayling Billy'. The last of the local steam railway engines was purchased by the brewers and placed in the pub's car park for some years, until given to the Isle of Wight Railway Society where it has since been restored and is running again, although its age is now over 100 years.

116. Tremendous changes have taken place here at Mengham. This road, now much wider, is Hayling's principal shopping area. The Black Hut, once the local fishmonger's shop, has gone and has been replaced by modern premises. With its removal, the district lost an old building of much charm and character.

117. Hayling Island is fortunate in still possessing many of its ancient farm buildings but progress has overtaken this example which stood for many years at Mengham. Mengham has now become the Island's principal shopping centre, catering for the needs of the growing number of holiday visitors as well as its local population.

118. A puzzle is posed in this postcard of Commercial Road in South Hayling. The decorative railings and much of the flint walling have gone, but the location can easily be recognised as South Road. The question must be asked as to why the original name was Commercial Road, for in 1907, the year of the photograph, Hayling Island had no commercial centre. Today, the road remains purely residential with the exception of the Island's police headquarters which is sited there.

Beach Road, Hayling Island.

119. Looking south from the junction of Beach, Manor, Station and St. Mary's Roads the appearance is almost that of a country lane; in 1924, it was, of course, little more, even though this was the main road to the sea. The houses on the right remain today, but the shop has disappeared and the road is now three times the width of the old thoroughfare.

120. The local celebrations to commemorate the Diamond Jubilee of Queen Victoria in 1897, included the erection of a drinking fountain on the corner of Beach Road and Seafront Road, its inscription reading: 'She brought her people lasting good.' The Hayling celebrations also involved the planting of sixty chestnut trees in nearby Victoria Avenue. Just one year later, the Victoria Hall was opened in Beach Road and named as a further tribute to those 'Sixty Glorious Years'.

121. Hayling's rustic influence still shows in the most surprising places and here in Station Road can be seen this traditional black weatherboarded barn. This view of 1917 shows a building which is unchanged today, although it is sited at the kerbside of a busy road and subjected to the continued rumbling of heavy traffic in addition to the vagaries of the coastal weather.

STATION ROAD AND STAUNTON AVENUE, SOUTH HAYLING.

BURROW, PUBLISHER, CHELTENHAM

122. Staunton Avenue in 1908 stretches away towards the seashore and is without houses. Named after an owner of the Leigh Park Estate, near Havant, it was at this time, like most of Hayling, undeveloped, and remained so for about another thirty years. The large house and shop premises still dominate this corner in Station Road and has been known for most of its years as the 'Station Stores' facing, as it did, Hayling's Railway station.

123. Shown here is Hayling Railway station and, surprisingly for a passenger service, there are no buffer stops at the lines end. Surely not an omission, so perhaps alterations were being undertaken at the time of this photograph which is of 1917 vintage. In the very early days of the Hayling Railway it was intended to extend the line as far as Sinah. There, the train would then continue either by bridge or floating bridge to the Portsmouth shore finally linking with the Portsmouth to East Southsea line at Fratton, thereby creating a circular rail system – Portsmouth, Havant, Hayling Island.

124. A mistake by the printer wrongly captioned this scene as 'The Ferry, Hayling' — easily excused, it shows, in fact, the Hayling Ferry Boat at its Portsmouth berth. The shoreline behind the pontoon is that of Milton, and the buildings of the Langstone Sanatorium can be faintly seen. The sailing barges are of particular interest; they plied from Velder Creek at Milton and were used for transporting shingle which was dug and loaded by hand whilst the vessels were beached on the Hayling shore or the Winner Bank. Hayling shingle has been used in most of the major road and building projects in the area for at least 100 years.

Golf House, Hayling Island.

125. Founded by the Sandeman family in 1883, the Hayling Island Golf Club has in very recent years celebrated its hundredth anniversary. The club's headquarters, originally no more than a hutment, soon progressed to grander premises and the building shown here is a result of the success of those early years. The course has always been acknowledged as one of the finest on the south coast and, with its continued popularity and growing membership, new and larger premises were again necessary. The present club house and headquarters, together comprise possibly the largest and most up to date golf club complex in the southern counties.

BEACHLAND LODGE, SOUTH HAYLING 1866

126. During the early years of the nineteenth century, attempts were made by the local 'Squirearchy' to ensure for Hayling a reputation as a watering place, containing all the amenities expected of such a resort. Grand hotels were envisaged and large, extravagant houses were erected in the southern half of the island. Attractions were to include a bath house, billiards room, coffee lounges, etc. Amongst a list of attractions there were pursuits such as riding, shooting and fishing, and the entrepreneurs built a library (later called Beachland Lodge), which contained a games room, a reading room and an art gallery. The intended plan to present Hayling Island to the world as another Bath or Cheltenham failed, in part, because of the planners choice in building: *Upon a shore where the south west wind sets almost continually for nine out of the twelve months of the year.* (Longcroft 1857.)

Cafe and Pony Stand, Hayling Island.

127. The Library, standing isolated on the shore, became part of a different holiday scene when the masses were encouraged to holiday at Hayling. Ices, soft drinks and confectionary were sold from here and it became a base for local donkey rides. This imposing building with its neo-classical Ionic columns, has now been demolished and, in its place stands a small brick built ice cream kiosk.

128. This junction of Beach Road and Seafront Road is, during the Season, Hayling's busiest holiday centre. It was originally the location of the Bath House, seen here in 1920. It has, for many years, been the home of the local fun fair and a variety of shops, cafés, restaurants and night clubs. Holidaymakers are naturally drawn to this area which is in the centre of the island's seafront.

129. The Bath House, which stood close to the shore and very near to the Royal Hotel, provided hot and cold sea water baths for those who did not favour sea bathing but wished, nevertheless, to enjoy a salt water 'soak'. Victorian prudishness may have been responsible for people's reluctance to bathe in public. At a slightly later date bathing machines were placed on the nearby beach to enable 'decent folk' to enjoy the delights of sea bathing whilst still preserving their modesty. Like its near neighbour, the Library, the Bath House also became a beach café and remained so until its demolition.

The Crescent, Hayling Island.

130. Part of a grand nineteenth century vision. 'The Crescent' is seemingly out of character with all but its neighbour the Royal Hotel. One can understand the planners intentions when comparisons are made with the extensive range of similar buildings which face the promenade and seafront at Brighton. It was hoped with the building of a bridge to the island in 1824 and the later opening of a railway in 1867, that Hayling would further develop and become a serious contender to its rival along the coast in Sussex.

131. Unfortunately, the incident depicted in this remarkable picture has not been recorded locally and, therefore, the reason is not known why this very early aeroplane should have come to rest so near to 'The Crescent' in South Hayling. Research has, however, shown the machine to be the 'Bristol Box Kite' No. 19, built in 1911 and sold to the Russians as a military aircraft. Transported to St. Petersburg, it was later returned to Britain as part of an exchange deal and was based at the Larkhill Flying School. Rebuilt and re-numbered No. 134, it crashed at Brooklands in November 1913. Here in this undated photograph, it is seen surrounded by interested spectators who are probably viewing a flying machine for the first time.

132. The year of 1825 saw work commence on what was almost certainly Hayling's first purpose built hotel. The Royal Hotel, still commands magnificent views of Hayling Bay, the eastern Isle of Wight and shipping using Spithead. In 1825, many vessels were still under sail and the Navy's ships would have presented a fine sight to guests who were staying there. The property today is owned by the London Borough of Tower Hamlets and provides holiday accommodation for the elderly folk of that Borough.

133. At least seventy years have passed since this postcard was produced and yet the scene remains almost unchanged. The local family butcher's shop retains its original appearance and the name of 'Twine' is still displayed above the window. Customer's purchases, alas, are no longer delivered by the attractive pony cart pictured here or, in the case of the neighbouring grocer, by his box tricycle. The decorative balustrade above the grocers is today covered by panelling but Seafront Road remains substantially as it is seen in this view.

Grand Hotel, South Hayling. 6033.

134. Probably the most impressive building to be seen at Hayling is this property currently in use as a private school. Originally built as a home for the well-known Sandeman family, it was known as Westfield House until late in the nineteenth century when, after conversion, it became the Grand Hotel. The intended development of the island as a first class resort never came about and the building enjoyed only a brief interlude as a hotel before it became the 'Chateau Blanc' Girls School. In the 1930's, it followed a trend set by advanced educationalists and became home to the Open-Air School of St. Patrick.

135. On this man made tropical island, monkeys ran free over the rocks and palm trees and were a delight to holidaymakers in the years before the Second World War. Dated 1934, this postcard shows the familiar 'pop-pop' boats with their paraffin engines, always smelly and very slow. So slow in fact, that the gentleman on the extreme right thought it quicker to get out and push!

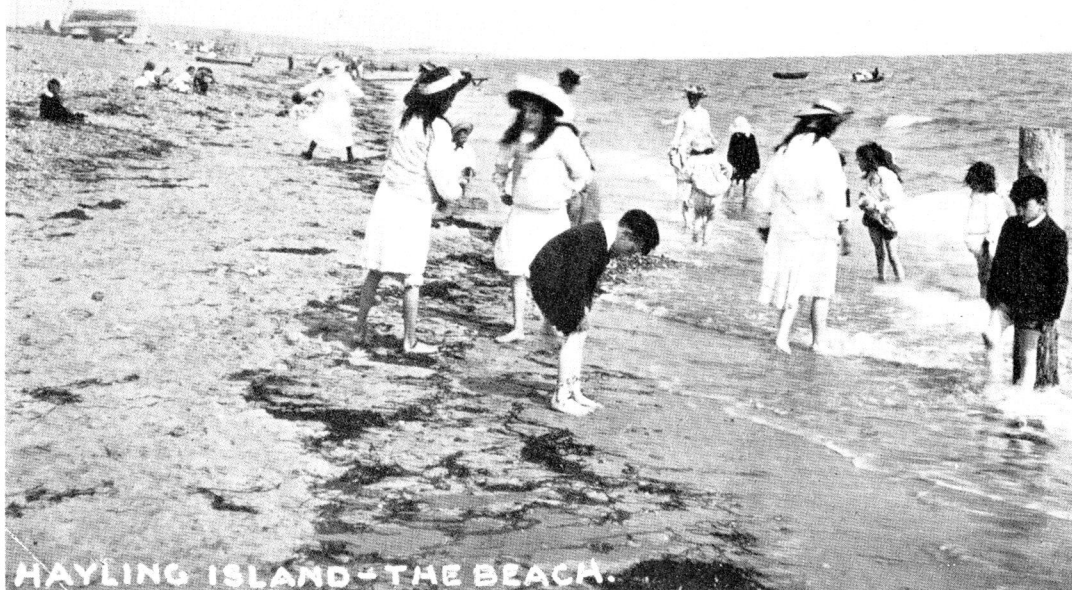

HAYLING ISLAND - THE BEACH.

136. Hayling's south beach in the early years of this century portrays the seaside styles of the period. Everyone present is almost fully clothed and appear to be positively over-dressed for the occasion, although they have abandoned their stockings! The shingle beach, shelving as it does towards the water, gives some idea of the difficulties experienced when launching and recovering the local lifeboat.

137. The 'Olive Leaf' public house commemorates the name of Hayling's first lifeboat which was donated to the Service in 1865, by the London company of Thomas Leaf and Sons. William Goldsmith, the first landlord, was also coxwain of the lifeboat. The 'Olive Leaf' lifeboat, powered by ten oars and Hayling muscle, is credited with saving 32 lives during its 23 years of service with the Hayling Island Station of the R.N.L.I.

138. The 'Lifeboat' public house, a near neighbour, is said to have been built at the same time as the 'Olive Leaf'. Tradition tells us of the race to complete the buildings and serve the first customer but it is not recorded which pub in fact won the day. The Hayling Life Boat Service was withdrawn in 1924 when the stations at Bembridge and Selsey, with their motorised vessels, took over the sea areas previously served by the Hayling crews.

The Hayling Island, Lifeboat

139. Although undated, this postcard of the Hayling Island Lifeboat is from the period 1888 to 1914 and shows the 'Charlie and Adrian' which saw service between these dates. It replaced, in 1888, the island's first official lifeboat the 'Olive Leaf', and was itself substituted by the 'Proctor' in 1914. The 'Charlie and Adrian' was donated to the Institute by L.T. Cave and during its service with the R.N.L.I. saved nine lives. The vessels always attracted a crowd when launched and those present in times of emergency often provided the muscle power necessary to put the boat into the water, there being no ramp or mechanical means of launching.

140. The 'Hayling Billy' locomotives, although often ridiculed in a most affectionate way, are much loved by all who knew them. This postcard gives a lighthearted impression of the local attitude towards the trains and is not to be taken seriously!